Ramsey Life Coaching

Road Map To Purchasing Your Dream Home

Sheri T. Ramsey

TABLE OF CONTENT

Introduction:

Congratulations in advance and best of wishes to you on your home buying journey! I hope this mini guide will be beneficial and assist you with achieving your goal of purchasing a home. Remember to stay consistent and do your research. This mini home buying manual will provide you with vital information to help you purchase a home. Also, provide a tip on how to purchase a home with out putting any money down. In addition, to receive money back by choosing a great realtor. I am confident if you create a goal plan after each part and set a goal with a date of completion you will purchase a home. Patience, Prayer, and Faith are the tools you need as you achieve an awesome goal in your life of purchasing a home. If you need assistance on your home buying journey schedule a life coaching session with me, Sheri T. Ramsey of Ramsey Life Coaching.

Part 1

Credit Score and Other Requirements

When you first consider purchasing a home it is vital to know your credit score. It is a good idea to have a credit score of at least 650. Most home buying programs or mortgage lenders will accept a 650 or higher. Your credit score dictates the types of mortgage loans that you qualify for and how much you will pay at closing. In addition, to your interest rate that will be added into your monthly mortgage payment. At this time if you have a good credit score you can qualify for an interest rate as low as 3.4%-4.0%. Your interest rate is also determined by how much money you put down. Remember the higher your credit scores the more loans you qualify to receive. The larger your down payment the lower interest rate you qualify to receive. The secret to not putting any money down on your home is to have a credit score of at least 700. Having a 700 plus credit score will help you to qualify for a 100% finance loan. Your interest rate will be slightly higher, but you will not have to put any money down upfront. Additionally you may ask the seller to pay the closing cost. You will not have to put any money down when you purchase your home and will have 45 days before you make your first mortgage payment.

Most mortgage lenders require that you be on your job for at least 2+ years. They are looking to verify the amount of years that you have been with the company and your income. If your employer has a contact line or email to verify your employment, secure that information now.

The amount of your mortgage is determined by the cost of the property you purchase, the taxes in the area, and the interest rate. A mortgage lender and a program have different rules and time frames to purchase a home. It's best to have good credit score of at least 700 or have a large amount of money to put down on the home if your credit is under

700.

Prior to contacting a mortgage lender or a home buying program have

a realtor secured and all the necessary documentation. **Have the contact**

information for your employer to verify employment. The mortgage lender

will also run your credit however, it is vital to know your own credit score.

In addition, they will ask for a copy of your bank statements and last 3

previous filed income taxes (W2's).

Goals

Write a list of all the documents you need for your mortgage loan application. Verify your credit Score. Create a daily to do list and review it at the end of each day. Set a deadline date to complete steps.

Ramsey Life Coaching Experience

Part 2

Saving For A Deposit And Closing Cost

When you first reach out to a realtor you have to give them a deposit that is referred to as earnest money. It is like a security deposit and it will go towards your closing cost. Typically, most realtors ask for a thousand dollars. Also, you may be required to pay all your closing cost that can range from 1-6% or more of the total cost of your home.

The down payment is due at the time of closing and most banks or other mortgage lenders companies require you to have the money already in your bank account. If you borrow the money from someone or it is given as a gift, than you will have to show proof from the person who sent you the gift. The amount of your closing cost is determined by many factors. When you purchase a home, it is good to negotiate if the seller can cover all or a portion of the closing cost. Try to save as much money as you can. Don't be afraid to negotiate. Negotiating is one of the keys to saving money during the home buying process. The most important key is to have good credit so that you can receive a low interest rate and qualify for good loans.

It is imperative to save as much money as you can on the purchase of your home, but you also want to save at least three to four thousand dollars for other cost outside of the closing cost and the deposit. The higher the cost of the home you purchase the more the closing cost will be. The location of your home and the taxes in the area will contribute largely to cost of your home which effects the appraisals of the home. Lastly, remember negotiation and saving at least 6 % of the cost of your home will be important to pay the upfront closing and deposit for the purchase of your home. However, you should have at least $3,000-5,000 saved for earnest money, home inspection, appraisal, the down payment and closing cost. Keep in mind the greater the cost of your home the more money that you will need to save.

Coaching tip: Purchase a home within your means and not at your means. Life happens your mortgage should be double the amount that you have saved or limit on your credit card. Saving for your down payment is what some people allow to defer them from purchasing a home. If saving the money is a hurdle for you than focus on getting your credit score to at least 650-700.

Part 3

Mortgage lender v.s Homeownership program

To purchase your home if you do not have the entire cost of the home upfront you will need a mortgage lender. Or some individuals may choose to purchase their home through a home ownership program. The way you choose to finance your home is up to you. However, there are a few key factors that you must qualify for if you choose to use a lender or go through a home buying program. A mortgage lender process will be faster than going through a home ownership program. Some realtors may know of some down payment assistant programs as they change rapidly.

A mortgage lender is a bank loan that pays for your house upfront and then you pay the loan back to the bank which is called your mortgage. Banks and some direct mortgage companies will loan you the money to pay for your house and then they will create a break down for you to pay the house off over a period of time. Most loans are 30-year loans depending on the interest rate and the cost of the home. The taxes and insurance of your home will all be calculated into your mortgage that you pay each month to the mortgage lender.

Mortgage Lenders have different loans that you can qualify for depending on your credit score and your income. A few Mortgage lenders are the major banks, credit unions and some companies that only do mortgage loans. (Verbal life coach session includes recommendations for mortgage companies, banks and credit unions). Each mortgage company offer different types of loans, the bank and credit unions offer different types of loans. Many of them have the same requirements. As stated in part one they require a lengthy job and rental history. Also, your income is factored into the type of mortgage loan that you will qualify to receive. It is vital to contact various mortgage lenders and choose the best loan.

A few home buying programs are habitat for humanity's, FHA, HUD, state workers, government workers, veterans and more. (Over the phone life coach session includes recommendations for home buying programs including contacts for some of the programs).

Home buying programs will purchase or build the home for you or may already own the home in some cases. You will pay your mortgage to the home buying company. In comparison to the mortgage lenders they also charge various interest rates and fees that are factored into your mortgage payments. Your credit score, rental, job history and income are all major components to qualify for these programs. Often times they allow you to volunteer and receive a discount on your home depending on the program.

One of the major differences between a mortgage lender and these types of programs are the credit score requirements are often less than mortgage lenders. Home buying programs may have more restrictions on the areas that you may purchase or build a home. Mainly they may take longer to qualify you for the program than receiving a loan from a mortgage lender. A benefit of using a mortgage lender is that you have more choices. The financial source that you use to purchase your home depends on your individual circumstances. Research the qualifications for the mortgage lender and the home buying program. It will help you to determine which financial institution is suitable for you. Select your lender wisely because you will have to pay them for 15 or 30 years depending on the amount of your home loan and down payment.

Goals

Verify the amount of money that you have saved. Set a budget. Research various mortgage lenders and home buy ownership programs, write qualifications. Create a daily to do list and review it at the end of each day. Set a deadline date to complete steps.

Ramsey Life Coaching Experience

Part 4
Realtors Are Key

After you have verified that you meet all the qualifications to purchase a home after working with a mortgage lender or researching various home buying programs the next step is to choose a realtor. They're many realtors and choosing one to assist you with purchasing your home is one of the most important steps. They will take precedent with facilitating the purchase of your dream home. Your realtor will work with the sellers and recommend properties to you based on your desires. They will assist with the negotiation of the cost of the home and closing cost. The realtor is responsible for making your home buying process stress free.

You can locate a variety of realtors online or sometimes mortgage lenders may refer you to a realtor program. If you know someone that is a realtor, it is good to utilize them as a resource. The experience of the realtor and their network is important. If they have a relationship with other sellers, they may have a better chance of negotiating certain terms. For example, if they're multiple bidders on the same property the realtor may have a good relationship with the seller, it could possibility work in your favor. Keep in mind the type of loan that you have also could work in your favor when there are multiple bidders. The realtor is vital as they play the middle man between you and the seller.

Some mortgage companies have programs that will assist you with securing a realtor. Some of these programs will give you an incentive for using their program. It is free money back in your pocket after you close on your home. (Ask me how in your free 45-minute home buying coaching session.) The realtor is paid during the closing of your home, they will receive a percentage of your home price. But don't worry you do not have to pay them out of your pocket. The realtor does not give you your mortgage loan that is given by the mortgage lender. The realtor will contact your mortgage lender once you have chosen a home that you would like to purchase. You will also need to inform your mortgage lender when you would like to put an offer in on a home. Your mortgage lender will provide you a breakdown of your monthly mortgage cost and have you to sign off on the loan. The realtor will send you all contracts to sign once you and the seller verbally agree on the sale. The realtor will arrange a meeting for closing with you, the realtor, the seller, and a lawyer to exchange payments from the mortgage lender and any other checks.

If you must pay any money at closing, you will need to have this money at the time of closing. If you will be receiving any money back at the time of closing the lawyer will have your check ready at that time. The realtor will then provide you your keys after all the documents are signed and money is exchanged. Your realtor is your voice it is crucial to choose someone that is professional, communicates effectively and you can trust.

Goals

Research realtors and write down questions to ask in your Free Life Coach Session. Write down a deadline to complete steps. Create a daily to do list and review it at the end of each day.

Ramsey Life Coaching Experience

SECURING THE KEYS

RAMSEY LIFE COACHING 90 DAYS DETAILED PLAN

This manual has provided a brief and detailed outline of the key components required to purchase a home. If you follow this 90 day plan it will enable you to be able to purchase a home in 90 days.

You hold the key to achieving this goal by being diligent, consistent, proactive, and remaining positive. Discipline is vital to achieve any goals.

Create a daily todo list it will help you to hold yourself accountable. If you need assistance with being held accountable hire me as your life coach.

Sessions are $15 per hours for coaching on purchasing your home.

90 Day Plan

MONTH 1: To purchase a home in 90 days you must use a MORTAGE LENDER NOT a HOMEBUYING PROGRAM. To get started verify that you have met all the requirements to purchase a home. Ensure that you have researched if you meet the qualifications from a mortgage lender. Also, have all documents that you need for your application process to qualify for a mortgage lender readily available. These documents include your previous year's taxes, W2's, bank statements, pay check stubs, employment verification number or email, identification, and social security card. If you are purchasing the home with someone they will also need this documentation. Research various mortgage lenders and banks online or give them a call inquire about the credit score requirements and the types of loans they offer, pay attention to the interest rates. Write down the details of each, create a plus and deltas chart. Choose a mortgage lender and home insurance company in the first 30 days. Submit your application, have all your documents ready to submit. Ensure that all your savings are intact.

MONTH 2: The next 30 days are important because you will need to secure a realtor. At this time, you should already know how much of a loan you qualify for or if you would like to use a home buying program. It is time to secure a realtor and start to look for homes. It is important to research the area that you would like to purchase your home before contacting the realtor it will make it easier to narrow down homes. Once you contact your realtor they will ask you questions regarding the type of home you are looking to purchase and will provide a list or website that you can research homes for sale. Also, you will need to give them a money order with your earnest money to begin the process.

Once you choose about 7 homes to view you will set up a day to meet with your realtor to view the homes. They will coordinate with the seller so that you can view the home. When you are viewing the homes make sure to look for water spots for possible leaks, flooding, mold, roof

life, heating and air units, and if appliances are included. It's ok to flush the

toilets and turn on the shower if the water is on. You will have to get a

home inspection before you move in your home you are responsible for

covering the cost of the inspection. They will check for termite's, rodents,

Ect. It's good to also look for signs of pest infestation. The inspection and

appraisal will need to be schedule once you choose the home you would like

to purchase and sign the purchase agreements between you and the seller.

MONTH 3: After viewing several homes hopefully one of them

is your dream home. Don't get frustrated with the selecting process, you

will know when you have found "The One". If you think the price is high,

then this is the time to negotiate with your realtor. The house will be

appraised to ensure that the house is being sold at the appropriate cost. You

will have to pay for the appraisals as well.

Once you have scheduled and paid for the house to be inspected and appraised it must pass state requirements. Anything that doesn't pass the seller will have to repair at his cost. Lastly, each department from the mortgage lender has signed off on your loan, then the mortgage lender will send the check to the lawyer. The realtor will secure a lawyer to seal the deal. A closing date will be determined by you, the seller, realtor and lawyer. A lawyer will receive the check from the bank and make all pay outs at the time of closing to the realtor, seller and yourself if you receive money back. This process is considering the closing process. It takes about an hour. (Yay, its almost over!)

If you owe any money at closing, you will need to have that money at this time. The mortgage lender and realtor will verify that you have the money prior to closing day. It is best to have this money in your account months prior to purchasing your home. The keys are exchanged after the funds are distributed. It's time to rejoice and breath the dream is real. Take the time to pat yourself on the back for achieving this accomplishment.

The key to home ownership in 90 days are in your reach if you have at least a 650-credit score preferably a 700-credit score, employed 3+ years and have at least 3,000 saved with no recent repo's or bankruptcies'. Have an idea of the location you would like to purchase your home. Ramsey Life Coaching can assist you with achieving this goal in 90 days, for a well spent fee of $60 which includes one bi weekly 75mins phone sessions for 90 days and a monthly detailed goal maps. Each session is $15 each. For purchasing this manual, you receive one free 45mins phone home buying coaching session. I look forward to helping you achieve your goal of homeownership.

Goals

Congratulations in advance on achieving your goal of home ownership. If you reach a road block along the way Ramsey Life Coaching is here to assist. Email *RamseyLifeCoaching@gmail.com* to schedule your home buying life coach session. You will receive one 45 minute session for free.

Ramsey Life Coaching